★ ★

EXPLORERS OF AMERICA

Coronado

EXPLORER OF THE SOUTHWEST

MATTHEW G. GRANT

Illustrated by Harold Henriksen

GALLERY OF GREAT AMERICANS SERIES

★ ★

Coronado

EXPLORER OF THE SOUTHWEST

Library of Congress Number: 73-13957   ISBN: 0-87191-285-6

Published by Creative Education, Mankato, Minnesota 56001

LIBRARY OF CONGRESS CATALOGING IN PUBLICATION DATA
Grant, Matthew G
  Coronado; explorer of the Southwest.

  (Explorers in America) (Gallery of great Americans series)
  SUMMARY: A brief biography of the Spanish explorers who led an expedition into the American Southwest in search of Gran Quivira and the seven cities of Cibola.
  1. Vazquez de Coronado, Francisco, 1510-1549—Juvenile literature.   [1. Coronado, Francisco Vasquez de, 1510-1554. 2. Explorers, Spanish. 3. America—Discovery and exploration]
I. Henriksen, Harold, illus. II. Title: Explorer of the Southwest.
E125.V3G72 973.1'6'0924 [B] [92] ISBN 0-87191-285-6 73-13957

CONTENTS

TALES OF GOLD 7

TROUBLE ON THE WAY 14

EXPLORATION OF CIBOLA 19

THE RICHES OF QUIVIRA 26

TALES OF GOLD

Four men came to the Viceroy of New Spain, Antonio de Mendoza, in 1536. For eight years they had been lost in the wilderness. They told a story about seven cities of gold, which lay somewhere north of Mexico City.

The Viceroy himself had only just come to New Spain. Cortes had taken the country away from the Aztec Indians in 1521. The

golden treasure of the Aztecs had lured many Spaniards to the New World. A poor soldier named Pizarro had found a second vast treasure in Peru, the land of the Incas. Now the Viceroy hoped to find still a third land of great wealth. He sent a priest, Friar Marcos, to explore the northern lands.

Friar Marcos visited what is now New Mexico. From a distance he saw what looked like a shining city. It seemed to him that the

place ought to have gold. Indian troubles forced Friar Marcos to return to Mexico. But his story of the "City of Cibola" was very exciting.

Viceroy Mendoza decided to send his most trusted official in search of the gold. The man he chose was Francisco Vasquez de Coronado.

Coronado was a poor Spanish noble-man — one of many who had come to seek his fortune in the New World. He was born in 1510 and came to Mexico in 1535 with the Viceroy. He may have been a relative. At any rate, the Viceroy saw that Coronado married a rich woman. Then, in 1538, Coronado was made Governor of New Galicia — now the Mexican state of Jalisco. He seems to have been brave and well-liked, but hardly destined to be a great explorer.

His great adventure seems to have been an accident of history. He did not go out on his own, as Pizarro and De Soto had done. He had no dream of glory like Columbus. Coronado was given a job to do, and he simply did it.

On February 23, 1540, his expedition set out from Compostela, Mexico. There were

about 300 soldiers and gentlemen, another
500 Indian servants, some priests, and a vast
number of horses, mules, cattle, and sheep.

TROUBLE ON THE WAY

They were only about 100 miles out,
still in country that was supposed to be

peaceful, when one officer was killed by an Indian arrow. It was only a hint of what lay ahead of them.

The vast army, guided by Friar Marcos, moved slowly through the rough country. Food ran short. Baggage was lost or thrown away by the tired servants. They suffered from heat, thirst, and weariness.

The journey to Cibola was 1,500 miles long. They finally reached their goal in July.

But instead of a beautiful city, they found only a walled pueblo village, built of mud and stones.

Well-armed Indians refused to allow the Spaniards to enter. Coronado's men were starving and desperate. He ordered them to

attack. The cannon, crossbows and muskets of the Spaniards soon overcame the brave Zuñi Indians, who fled.

Coronado's expedition entered the pueblo. They found no gold — but there was food at any rate. So they thanked God.

EXPLORATION OF CIBOLA

Where were the seven cities of gold? Coronado sent parties out to explore the "Land of Cibola." In the meantime, Friar

Marcos was lucky to escape with his life. The men blamed the fiasco on him.

One group of Spanish scouts visited the Hopi pueblos to the northwest. They found no gold. A captain named Garcia Lopez de Cardenas came back with a fantastic story. He swore he had seen a mighty gorge, with a river so deep inside that it seemed like only a silver thread.

Everyone laughed at Cardenas. They could not know that he had discovered the Grand Canyon.

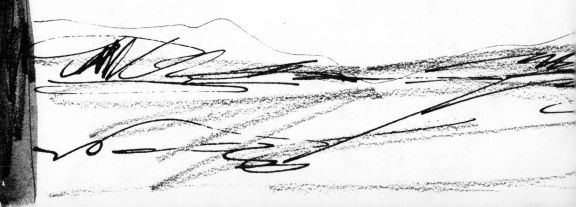

Another captain, Hernando de Alvarado, went eastward into Texas. He saw herds of huge "hump-backed oxen." They were the buffalo of the Great Plains.

In August Coronado sent a sad letter to the Viceroy: "The Seven Cities are only seven little villages . . . . There does not appear to be any hope of finding either gold or silver."

But he intended to keep on searching.

Coronado spent the winter of 1540-41 in a village on the Rio Grande called Tiguex. He was there when Captain Alvarado rode in with great news. An Indian from the North, held captive by a Texas tribe, had told him of a country called Quivira, which was full of gold! Alvarado brought with him the Indian captive, who was nicknamed the Turk because of his shaved head.

The Turk said he would guide Coronado to Quivira.

In April, 1541, Coronado and his army set out for Quivira. The men were happy and full of hope. The Turk told them that it was not too far away. He told them that the king of Quivira rode in a golden boat and the people ate from golden dishes.

And as he spun his tale, he led the army into the desolate Staked Plains of Texas. A second Indian guide, Isopete, told Coronado they were going the wrong way.

The Turk had to confess. The Pueblo Indians had promised to let him go free if he took the Spaniards into the wilderness and lost them. Coronado was furious but still hoped to find Quivira.

He sent the main army back to wait at Tiguex. He picked 30 horsemen and six foot-soldiers to go North with him in search of the City of Gold. Isopete led them. The Turk, in chains, followed behind.

THE RICHES OF QUIVIRA

They had a magnetized needle, hung from a silk thread. This simple tool pointed the way to Quivira. They traveled for 30 days, following a trail made by buffalo, and came to the Arkansas River.

Isopete told them that beyond the river lay his homeland, Quivira. And as he had also told them, the country was beautiful, with fertile soil and peaceful people — Indians now called the Wichita tribe.

But there was no gold. The Turk urged the people of Quivira to murder the Spaniards. Disgusted, Coronado had him executed.

Then he solemnly claimed the land for Spain.
The Wichitas just smiled.

It was August. Soon the autumn would
come and then the winter. The Wichitas pro-
vided Coronado with guides to
lead him back

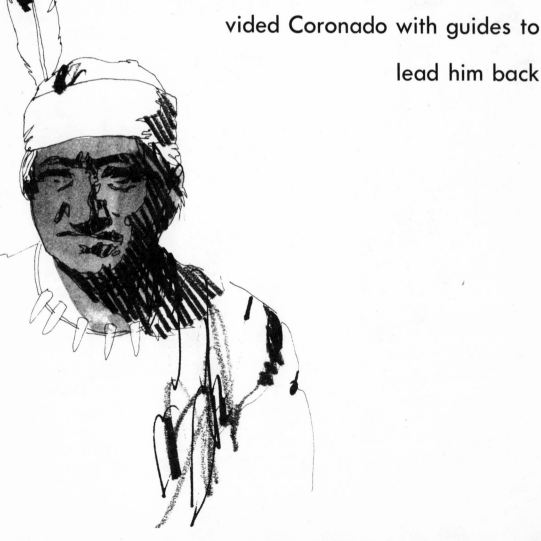

to where he had come from. He returned to Tiguex and prepared to spend the winter with his men.

In December, he suffered a head injury in a fall from a horse. Confused and in

pain, he began to long for his wife and home in Mexico. The next spring he led the army home. The priests stayed to convert the Indians.

Coronado had not found the treasure he expected. But because of his exploration, Spain claimed a new part of the world and began to settle it.

With his job done, Coronado resumed his governing of New Galicia. In 1544 he was removed for neglect of duty and spent the rest of his life as *regidor*, or alderman, in Mexico City. He died peacefully in bed in 1554, only 44 years old.

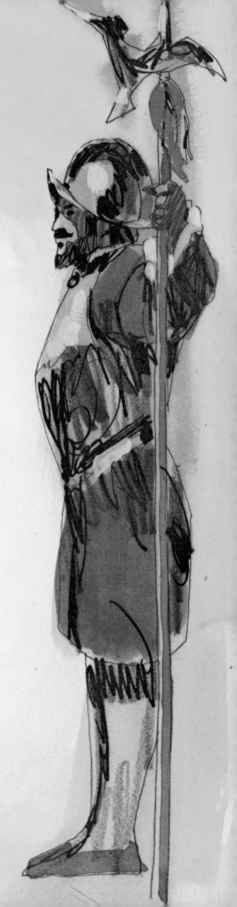

★ ★

GALLERY OF GREAT AMERICANS SERIES

★ ★

INDIANS OF AMERICA
- GERONIMO
- CRAZY HORSE
- CHIEF JOSEPH
- PONTIAC
- SQUANTO
- OSCEOLA

EXPLORERS OF AMERICA
- COLUMBUS
- LEIF ERICSON
- DeSOTO
- LEWIS AND CLARK
- CHAMPLAIN
- CORONADO

FRONTIERSMEN OF AMERICA
- DANIEL BOONE
- BUFFALO BILL
- JIM BRIDGER
- FRANCIS MARION
- DAVY CROCKETT
- KIT CARSON

WAR HEROES OF AMERICA
- JOHN PAUL JONES
- PAUL REVERE
- ROBERT E. LEE
- ULYSSES S. GRANT
- SAM HOUSTON
- LAFAYETTE

WOMEN OF AMERICA
- CLARA BARTON
- JANE ADDAMS
- ELIZABETH BLACKWELL
- HARRIET TUBMAN
- SUSAN B. ANTHONY
- DOLLEY MADISON

★ ★